I0616684

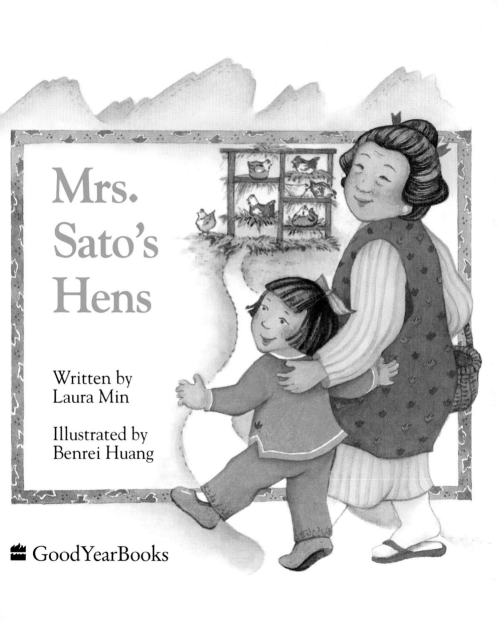

Mrs. Sato's Hens

Written by
Laura Min

Illustrated by
Benrei Huang

GoodYearBooks

On Sunday I went to see
Mrs. Sato's hens.

2

On Monday we counted
two white eggs.

On Tuesday we counted
three brown eggs.

On Wednesday we counted
four speckled eggs.

On Thursday we counted
five small eggs.

On Friday we counted
six big eggs.

On Saturday we didn't count
any eggs.